Star Route

Creston, W VA 26141
1973
Letters and Stories

Johnny Lyons

Direct inquiries to:
2 Pups Enterprises
PO Box 42
Lecompton, KS 66050

Printed in USA

First printing 2021

ISBN 978-1-7335472-3-9

For Bobby and Bevie

OPENINGS

I came across an Old Folder this winter, that
contained 32 letters I had sent my Dad during
1973 and 1975, when I was living on the
Communal Farm in West Virginia.
I had been searching around for the next writing
project, after publishing "Rowells Run" (gleanings
from the Journals I kept at the time).
Being such a pivotal and exciting time for me, I
knew there were so many more
stories and tales that wanted to be told, I
just wasn't sure how.
It was the week of my 70th Birthday I found the
letters – there are No Coincidences.

The relationship with my Dad was forged deeply
while we grew together
after my Mom passed in 1965 ~ I was just 15.
Through 8 years of High School, Junior College
and State University
we grew together and apart.

These are The Transcribed Letters I sent him in
1973 from the Farm.
I held myself back, and did not change a word.
Within Each Letter, I found Touchstones of
Memories and Stories

Some of which are included, as well as a Journey I made that summer.

I was still wondering about the title for this collection when I realized "it's there in the address".

Star Route was the Original name given to our postal route. My reaction to this name, was the same as I had back in 1973:

"Far Out".

I hope you enjoy and feel free to drop a line – **jwlyons3249@gmail.com.**

Himself
November 2020
Lawrence, Kansas

These from Me, He kept

Touching the Letter
Feeling the Dust of years,   nearly fifty
Smelling the smells of years long gone,
    now refreshed
Reading and Hearing the Love given ~
    received at every lines end.

How oft' were these words and lines read?
    These dated pages he kept.

There is Sunlight and Care there
        still upon the pages, envelopes and stamps.

Opened envelopes stapled to the back of pages
        each placed and packed away.

These from me, he kept for me   forever.

Jwl 2/14/20

Weds. Night

Dear Dad,

I am sitting here with kerosene lamp, the pot-belly stove a blazin' warm. Had a real nice time today. I woke up about 6:30 in the mornin'. Cut wood, made a fire in the stove, went down to the stream to bathe, made coffee and in comes Gordy our neighbor who has mules~

he said "well, lets get to work... I'll go get the mules and wagon and we'll go get the cookstove (which we bought from an old farmer about 3 miles away for $15!).

I went with him, took the mules to the stream for water, and then we hooked up the wagon and rode to the place where they had the stove ~ it sure was fun drivin' the mules, riding through the beautiful mountains and trees all around~ and dirt roads!

Tomorrow he's coming to help us plow a potato and onion patch with the mules - they are really big animals - as big as horses but gentle as kittens. Gordy has been a real help to us. He's such a fine person. We get over a gallon of milk a day from his cow - "Chocolate" (not milk- that's her name) and a dozen eggs every few days.

He lent us his Bible last night. Rona and I went up for milk and we sat in his cabin and talked for about two hours about life and the scripture. One winter he read the bible twice.

He said "They're good words to think about while you're workin'...

The country here is so beautiful. So many mountains and trees and real good people who are always willing to help you out. Yesterday we went to the highway dep't to see if they could come and fix our road. They were here the next day (today) working real hard.

It's real hard work starting a farm. There are so many things to do. Basically all we have done is organize our living spaces and particulars about food, washing clothes, dishes and ourselves, gathering supplies and cutting enough wood to keep warm.

Now , that all of that is basically done ~ we'll begin ploughing, planting, fixing the food shed, chicken shed, digging and building an Out-house
(right now when we go to the bathroom we go out to a ditch and do it~ there's no time to sit and read like I used to because I'm afraid a woodchuck or raccoon will come up and bite me bottom!)

5

The weather here has been periodically rainy. Mixed in with sun. Today it was cloudy all day until about 3 pm- then sunshine came, until it went down.

The most beautiful morning was the first one I saw here. It rained all night (on tin roofs-it sounds like the flood Noah had!) anyway, in the morning steam and fog all up and down the valley, and the sun shining through. It was gorgeous.

One afternoon a few days ago it began to rain and right across the valley we are in, a big rainbow arching from north to south ~ it made me wonder if we are inside the gates of heaven, or just outside of them.

There are a lot of raccoons and woodchucks – which present a problem for us ~ They Love Gardens. Alot of deer, there are tracks all around the farm and after a rain, you can tell they come here at night.

Mice have found out about our presence. ~ we forgot one night to cover the milk, and found one floating in the morning...ugh – but we learned our lesson.

Well, it's up in the morning to plow a potato patch and I'm real tired- 'still have to write Karen and Marci.

Everytime I get into Grantsville, I

will give you a ring, I sure miss you and being near you. But it is only Land Distance.

There are a lot of Dogwood trees in bloom, they make me think of Mom. I'm going to plant one by the house for her and you.

Have Good Gentlr days and I will plant some potatoes for you.

Son John
p.s. Here's the correct address
John Lyons
Armadillo Farm
Star Route,
Creston, West Virginia 26141

GORDY GARRETSON

Gordy was our first and closest neighbor on Rowells Run.
We did not know of him until the day he came to our place
a day or so after we landed.
He was became a Mentor for me – teaching me how to
work a team of horses and mules, how to care for them,
everything from feeding and pasturage to shoe-ing to
building a wagon.
and of course--- to how to milk a cow.
A fine and helpful neighbor and a heartfelt friend.

Imagine for a minute:
The epitome of a "Hillbilly", 2 bedroom shack, snug back
in a West Virginia holler
– you come close to Gordy's "house" and birthplace.
Pure and Raw Appalachia
I cannot remember how old he was, or if he even told me.
Somehow I feel he was close in age to my Dad – so that
puts him around...
60 years
Gordy was a smallish wirey man, standing shorter than me
at 5' 8".
The times – Hard and Soft had chisled the marks on him
Tattoos from the "Merchant Marine- WWII" days had
faded.
My memory visualizes –
a cross between a Young Pappy from Lil' Abner and
Popeye the Sailorman
...but I'll not forget the Sparkly Glint in his eyes.
He lived alone, was married for a while, had a Daughter
(who I met one dark rainy night).

Both his parents were of Swedish Stock and settled the 50-
odd acre farm in the early 1900's.
After the War, through the 1940's Gordy found work in the
Coal-Mines,
became fond of The Drink – ending up with the Black-
Lung and Alcoholism.

Living off "the Pension" as he said,
he came back to the homestead.
Got him a horse, 2 mules, a milk cow and a flock of
chickens and lived alone.
Most days were fine, then he'd disappear – then sober up
and come home.

He never took drink on the farm -ever – because of his
mother.

When we first moved to our farm, he was a great help
setting us up with a cook-stove,
plowing garden patches, cut and harvest hay, with the team,
teaching me how to work with them
and getting a kick out of our company and my follies of
that, I'm certain.

"SAGA OF THE DOUBLE-TREES"

One day Gordy needed help fixing a fence-line to a pasture
way down the road – so he and I packed up the tools on
the flat-bed wagon
(made from the chassis of an old Model A Ford)
– hitched the team, and off we went.
Arriving at our destination, we unpacked the wagon,
un-hitched the team

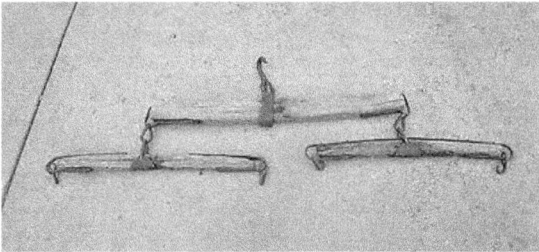

pretty accurate picture – all the harnessing Gordy had were ancient

In the process, the double-tree snapped in half and we were
dead in the water. But just for a moment.

Gordy's solution? I was to ride Jack
(the largest of the two mules)
back to his barn and get the "spare".
Now, I hadn't been on the farm but...2 weeks?
I'd never *seen*, let alone *ride* a mule
(or anything else but a bicycle for that matter).
There was no saddle.
Once I finally hefted myself on Jacks back, after a few circle
dances,
Gordy handed up the broken double-tree to take back.
So, with Jack's bridle clenched in one fist, holding the
double tree perilously to my lap,
Down the road we went.
Mules don't really run or gallop.
The experience is more like riding a Jack Hammer with
Four legs.
Not sure how, but I did manage to get to his barn,
get the spare,
re-mount and return.
....he's laughing still

April 6, 1973 Friday

A good early morning to y'all. Been awake about an hour now. The sun just beginning to rise. I woke up either because I was cold and wanted to start a fire, or I just had a good nights sleep. Rona and Jonathan are asleep still. We got to bed around 7 p.m just at nightfall. Spent a good days work on the farm yesterday. Cleaned up and tore down part of the root-cellar and dry house so we can begin to re-build; cleaned the chicken house, cut wood, made a foot-bridge, dug a latrine and cleaned up the yard.

The view here is really spectacular such beautiful space with beautiful mountains that are covered with budding and blooming trees. Alot of wild-flowers are in bloom now too. I have taken a few walks up the hollers and creek beds~ it is so wild and beautiful.

I can hardly believe that I am here. Gordy our neighbor says there are herds of 10 or twelve deer that live around here. In the morning sometimes you can see deer tracks. Alot of groundhogs, raccoons, birds and I guess the word is out that there's good eats at the old Metz place (that's what all the locals call this farm)

It's been raining for a day sporatically~ we were going to plow a Potato and Onion patch with Gordy and the mules, but we're going to have to wait until the ground dries up. Tomorrow we are going to Spencer for supplies if it still rains.

Gordy's milk cow Chocolate is
        expecting in August
We all hope she has a heifer!
        That's all for now,
                must get to the chores.

        Have Good Days and Keep Well.

        A lot of love from the mountains
         John

April 18, 1973   *pencil*
                              Tuesday night

  We just finished building the
"Summer Kitchen" (semi enclosed area to
keep the woodstove * see note)
We went up a ridge, cut down 4 Pitch Pine
to frame it up. Wood boards for a roof –
will cover with tar-paper. The sides will be
canvas so that on hot days we can roll
them up. Chickens come tomorrow, so we
spent time cleaning and re-building the
coop. We were going to plow the garden
today but it rained last night and off and
on all day.
  Two days ago I went for a walk in
the woods and scared up alot of wild
animals- coons, woodchucks, pheasant and
a wild turkey. I was really surprised. The
only I've ever seen is in the oven! We've
have some really nice weather for about 3
days~ I got sunburned digging hot frames.
(Hot frames are a square pit with board
around the sides- you put fresh manure in
the bottom (preferably Horse manure) –
cover with about 6-7 inches of soil keeping
the germinating seed warm from any
frost.)

Tomorrow Rona and I go into Spencer - which is about 40 miles away - for a water pump, tar paper and other supplies. I have begun making plans for a cabin in the woods. I found a spot and have a vague idea how to build it, but no specifics yet. I'll let you know how it will be coming. I'm listening to Beethoven on tape. Everyone is asleep.

Oh if you're out shopping and happen by a bookstore, could you pick up a copy of "Walden" by Henry D. Thoreau. Paperback should only be 50cs -$1.00.

Thanx for your letter- write more it is always good to hear from you

I love you keep well

Son John

* It dawned on us when preparing to set up the Wood-burning Cook stove... it probly would be a better idea to set it up Outside the house for the Summer. Without Electricity – Fans and Air conditioning weren't an option.

All The First Month

The Month of April Gathered Steam Daily
Survival Skills and Innovations Put to the Test
Growth and Expansion at Every Turn
There was Always Something and Someone New
By April's End
Working and Living Spaces Set To
Necessities and Priorities Established
Faint Green lines of Gardens Emerging
By Month's End and Early May our Numbers
Grew
Sixteen Fold
Gordy offered to sell his Stock
2 Mules   1 Draft Mare   1 Milk Cow   12 Chickens
1 Flat Bed Wagon, 1 Plow, 1 Disc, 1 Harrow, 1
Hay Mower and 2 Hay Rakes
All the Harnessing and Assorted Husbandry
Tools he had.

We had it goin' on
and All Who Wanted to Come
~ Came

and then some

jwl Sept 2020

May 10, 1973

Dear Dad,

Received your letter yesterday but it took
a while to get to me. Alan went to pick up
the mail and put the letters in his back
pocket. On his way back home- (it's a half-
mile to the mailbox) he climbed a mountain
and your letter go dropped along the way.
I was disc-ing the garden area with the
mules and afterward took Bob (a mule)
down the road (I rode him) to look for it.
Even with both of us looking- we both
didn't see it, so I took Bob back to the barn
and ate dinner. Afterwards, I climbed the
mountain and found it laying around in
the leaves. It was quite an adventure.
It was decided by the family that Gerry,
Jonathan and I should be the ones to take
care of the horse Dolly, the two mules Bob
and Jack, and the milk- cow Chocolate (It's
rather funny but every time I call Bob -
"Bobby" -I think of you!)
So, now I am learning to work the mules ~
disc-ing the garden- ploughing – and
harrowing.

When you disc, the team pulls a machine with big metal discs which are sharp and cut it up and turn ground.

When you harrow, they pull a frame of wood with spikes that drag over the ground and level up the ground that you turned over with the discs. It's all very exciting, and such a wonderful feeling to work the earth with animals. It really brings one "down to earth"

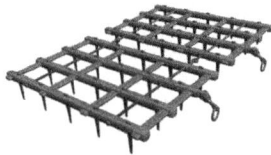

At present we have two roosters which wake us up at 5 in the morn, 24 hens, 7 chicks and a wild mallard duck that flew in one afternoon and decided to stay. I think He thinks he's a chicken, with food as a bribe he'll come within a yard of you- so beautiful. Enclosed is a picture of the farm (a print of the slides you saw). When we find the camera, I'll take a whole roll of pictures and send them to you. It is unbelievably beautiful here. All different kinds of wild birds and animals. I don't know if I told you but I saw a Red Fox up on a hill one late afternoon. That was really something.

So far we have planted potatoes, onions, carrots, kale, soybeans, collards and radishes. Pretty soon- the last expected frost date will come (May 20th). Then we can plant the majority of vegetables. I guess I told you on the phone about the chickens and how we ate them. I think my vegetarianism has it's bounds sometimes. The main thing is that I am very healthy and that's most important.

Your plans to move sound real fine. Let me know what you decide.

We are all incredibly busy here building a comfortable home and efficient farm. You wake up early in the morning and work til dark. Very tired everyone goes to bed. It is so much more rewarding than a job ~ always something new to do and knowing that we are planting and caring for the food we eat is quite a religious feeling. I feel quite in tune with the world and nature now more than ever which makes me very happy. I have just about all I need except a woman and my family near me which I truly miss but, you are near in my heart and my thoughts and prayers. Give my love to the neighbors, they may read this letter too if you like.

Send it off to Marci and Lee, so that I won't have to write so many times for it's hard and much better to catch two birds in one swipe.

    I love you, stay well
   gotta go water the mules
   Love,
     Son John

p.s. Thank you for the Easter card and the money. I am saving it to buy canvas for a "wiki-up" (a little hut to build in the woods) tell Marci & Lee to please drop a line this way.

  p.s.s for the first time tonight I milked a cow – how wonderful. It's stormy tonight, thunder lightning and a whole lot of rain. If you are having a whole lot of good, dry weather send some this way so's we can plant~

Marsha Mae and the Highway Department Boys

Our Road –
Only One Way In
Only One Way Out
-    the Perils of Living in a Holler.

The original road was 15 feet below Rock and Dirt
at the Holler's Floor
There were no clues how long ago this road, in and out,
was made, but it was carved out of the hillside
at least 20 years ago.
Ten foot Wide and a Quarter Mile long
to Gordy's Turn Off
(from there it was Bed Rock and Stream Beds
for another half mile
til you got to the Main "Star Route" Road & the Mail Box)

….can't say it was a Dirt Road or a Mud Road,
– it was both really,
and not designed for the traffic of 20+ people
and their Trucks.

I think It was happiest when Me & the Team made our
trips back & forth
and we'd have our conversations.

The Design, if you could call it that,
was Simple:

Dig it out of the Hillside –

A shelf, with a little ditch on the side - to carry the run off.

The road-bed was prob'ly not really maintained - if ever,
(and we never did get that Dirt Road Manual....)
so,........ with our back and forths

Big Green Ford Truck Ruts

Foot Prints, Boot Prints,

Groundhog, Raccoon, Fox and Turkey Prints
Hoof Prints,
Wagon Wheel Ruts,

a few good rains....

Welcome to:

THE MORASS HIGHWAY OF BOG

I didn't drive Cars or Trucks or Tractors in those days ~
Only the Team
Many was a Rainy Night when I was roused from my
slumbers
"Johnny – Get the Team – The Truck's in the Ditch..."
one of the jobs I got real good at.

In the early days we realised we had a problem,
so we stopped by the
Calhoun County Highway Department
to see if they could help us.

*Word travelled fast around here – no matter where we went -
people had heard of us – like the Circus had come to town.
Everyone was Very Kind and So Curious...*

The very next day - Back hoes, Graders, Front loaders and
Dump Trucks came parading Yellow
down the road with a 6-man crew.

We conferred the obvious problem and They set to work
Grading Filling Spreading Ditching
and all of us watching the spectacle unfold

Great Fun!

During one of the breaks in the action,
Marsha Mae asked them:

"...how can we make a Little Pond in the Stream over there
across the holler?"

Marsh Mae is a Beautiful Brown Haired Brown Eyed Lithe
Jazz Dancer from Up- State New York.

She could move like a waterfall

Those boys would have dug a Lake Ontario
for her that day. I'm certain.

The Pond was enjoyed for several Seasons
and was the site of

The Communal Bath and Sweat Lodge.

And the Road went on Forever ~

until it rained....

About the Chickens
and How We Ate Them in Mid- May

When Gordy decided to sell his Stock, Including Chickens,
he provided us with:

Challenge No. 1

How do you move 12 Good size Chickens
– without having cages??

Gordy's Idea was the Best Idea any of us had:

Get some Burlap Bags, Flashlights and wait til night.
Steal into the Coop
Stun them with Flashlight
Stuff Two or Three in a Sack
Carry them to the Coop on our Farm
Easy Peasy Kundalini
not quite
The Flashlight Stun Game was only Partially Effective.
There were 4 of us, plus Gordy.
The Coop only had room for two of us,
We could only find 5 Burlap Bags
It was Dark.
Cascading feathers, Shrieks of Terrified Chickens,
The Rustle of Burlap
and two Flashlights – one that didn't work.
Then, the transport by foot down the dirt road with
Squirming Burlap Bags of Chicken

It was Dark.

Seven of the Twelve Made it – that left Five deceased.

Chicken Stew! Roast Chicken! Chicken Delite! Chicken
and Beans!
(keep in mind, some of us were Vegetarian by Necessity
Only)

Challenge No. 2

Not One of us had ever De - Feathered a Chicken –
plucked or other wise.
I recalled reading about Boiling the Chicken First
or it might have been an Episode of Beverly Hillbillies

Put them to the Boil we did,
and Yanked Wet Feathers for hours.
Confirmed Vegetarians stood watching on the sidelines.
Gordy came by for the Chicken Feast.
He said "Brownie" tasted the Best.

I NEVER Wish to: See, Feel, Smell or Pluck or
Yank another Wet Feather as long as I lived.

Someone wanted to dry the feathers for pillows
yeah right

May 29, 1973

Dear Dad,
    I guess this has been a moving one for the both of us. Last week I built a Wiki-up Lodge in the woods to live in for the season until winter. A Wiki-Up is a dome like tent. Using tree saplings about 2"- 3" in diameter (Tulip Tree and Black Birch). I put them into the ground about a foot- in a circle. I bent them over to each other, so you have a simple dome- frame structure.
    Temporarily I have covered it with an old tent and plastic. It's pretty water tight. It rained last night and I didn't get wet. It is very nice~ gradually I will buy some canvas sheets and cover it and later make a floor of some sort. I haven't figured out that part yet.
    It's quite a ways up a the holler (a small valley between two mountains) about a 10 minute hike from the big house and mostly up hill. The ground is flat and a creek runs by down a slope about 4 yards out the door.
    I sleep in the sleeping bag you gave me, on a tarp so I dont lie directly on the ground. I made a little campfire spot out the door to cook tea or food if I ever want

to. It's very nice and feels good. Inside it's as high as I am and 10 feet from side to side - front to back. At maximum 3 or 4 can sleep in it. As much as 10 have sat in here around in a circle.

A long time ago the Sioux, Crow, Blackfeet Indians (and other Plains Indians) Single men lived in wiki-ups like me and only after they got married would they live in a TeePee, for a TeePee is a womans art. Well, I'm still single and waiting for a squaw to come along with a TeePee. Ha!

All is well, and drying up. Hopefully I will disk and Harrow the Big Garden with Jack and Bob. I will think of you - "Bobbie" sends his regards!

Hee- Haw

I am sure you are very busy settling in and very happy ~ change is a good thing.

I guess we can say another chapter~ we are very fortunate- life is good. I bless it everyday. I miss you and hold you in my heart. Sending energy to help you "un-pack" etc. You're an old hand at it though. Say hello to new neighbors and Jan and Bub, Marci and Lee.

Love from the mountains
and Son John

p.s. I milk the cow everyday. O how wonderful.

Many Hands Make Light Milk
and Chocolate has a Crush

It became rather evident early on, that we'll need more than
One person to milk "Chocolate"
-our lovely Brown Swiss Milk Cow - once she moved in.

Eloise was the only one on the farm who really knew how-
I was just learning, the Training wheels
(or buckets) were still on.
So with her coaching skill and Chocolate's forebearance,
I soon became a skilled milker
and Eloise and I became the "Morning Team"
me, taking the left side   her, the right.
Gerry and Jonathan eventually covered the evening shift.

We all found that milking in pairs is faster
and easier for all concerned.
I did so love the milking, the "Milk Scratches" and
early morning Barnlight.
And the O! So Fresh Warm Milk in the morning

In conjunction with this activity was the
"Who gets the Alarm Clock?" game.
I did not relish losing...

The next summer, I was gifted an old fiddle and I asked
Eloise to "learn me how"...

Eloise

… my milking buddy and fiddling coachette
Lawrence, Kansas around 2011

Now, Ken Dubie, Long Tall Extremely Laid back Texas
guy
was my pal and we both loved to go "Grazin' ".
We would Wander off exploring and trying to solve
The Mysteries of the Universe and Escaping the Personality
Struggles
that come with a Community of 20 people Co-existing.

One Day He looked Deep in My eyes and said:

"Johnny? Why Should I be Up-tight?"

…..a mantra I've carried with ever since.

...Coming home from one of our "grazin's" one afternoon,
we were crossing through a pasture
where Chocolate was "grazin'"

...and she saw Ken.
She loved Ken.

She bellowed and chased him around that pasture for a
good 10 minutes,

all the while he's trying to find the gate.

He barely escaped, the Audience that gathered cheered:

"Everybody Loves Ken Dubie!"

As a Safety measure,
Ken was not allowed on the Milking Teams.

June 5, 1973

Dear Marci, Lee and ? + All the family!

Greetings from West Virginia. Things are really buzzing around here ~ planting hoe-ing – hay-ing. Nobody can come to cut the hay for us so Gordy our neighbor taught us how to harvest with the horse and mule. Alot of hard work but very exciting. I learned how to plow with them the other day which was a real earthy experience. I hope you have been reading the letters I send to Dad and vice versa – that way I can give you all a good picture of what I've been doing. We have a Volley-ball court set up in the meadow and play every night after dinner (if it doesn't rain) it is really a lot of fun.
         Remember how I loved to chop wood at the lake?
Well, I must say I have become quite the expert with an axe. Do you get down there a lot? How is Papa Loom and the family? I think of you often and long to see your faces.
         Traveling this path I have learned quite a lot and grow more and more everyday - like the garden.
No harvesting yet but we pick wild greens

- sorrel, plantain, yellow clover, poke, and white top for salads and eat a lot of grain ~ tiresome but healthy and keeps us going. The 1st garden is almost totally planted in tomatoes, peppers, peas, greens, cauliflower broccoli, then the potato patches is ¾ acre of potatoes, more greens and we shall finish with melons.

The big Garden by the house 2 acres will be planted in field corn for the animal stock - more veggies and beans and melons. There is one more track of land that will be plowed this week for peanuts and more field corn. Oh and finally we will plow 1 more acre for sweet corn.

if it seems like a lot of land and work to you-
you are correct! But we are very happy and excited about it - a good honest rewarding way of life.

How are Jan and Bub and Kirk- send this on to them with my love. (Bub - we are going to make some home-brew - you can't get Genesee here - too bad.

Marci - tap your tummy for me! Love to hear from y'all.

All my love -
Brother John

HAY-TIMES

I had a Love / Hate Relationship with Lady Hay

It was a Hot Sweaty Itchy Dusty Exhausting task
from Beginning to End

Next to Water, this job was at the
Nexus of Everything else.

In all my 23 years, I never had to deal with, let
alone think about- hay. None of us did.

and Gordy was Delighted to teach us.

One of the Springtime -rainy day tasks,
was to Tune up all the Machines.
Lubricating the Mower and Sharpening the
Triangle- Teeth Blades was my favorite.
The Easier the working parts moved-
the Easier it will be for the team to pull.
Jonathan and Gerry took to the mowing a lot
faster
than I did- fine by me.
The team of the three of us worked well.

Raking the Windrows
Now this was fun!

Once we had the field mowed, and the hay was dry, we needed to rake the hay into rows to gather it.

We had Two rakes -
Gerry and I would have races around the field.

And Loading the Wagons

Once the hay was dried and Cured, we'd load the
hay and haul it to the Barn. I had added
"extenders" to the wagonbed
make the wagom wider for the hay,
by using Tulip Tree saplings –
laid over the bed.

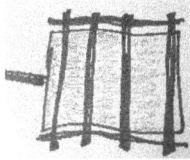

The Ultimate Hay Ride

So, we'd have the team pull the wagon though the
field, and we'd load the hay.
Under Gordy's supervision -
Layering it just so,
higher and higher making sure
the balance was even all around the wagon.
I remember seeing pictures,
but doin' this "live"... was a trip.

It wasn't recommended
to ride way up on top and drive.
So, I would stand at the very front,
with reins in hand and Go

Now- remember what I said about our road?
No Expressway Here.
Every Rut, Every Bump,
Every Stone in the Road was Magnified.
Like bein' at Sea in a Tub.

The Wagon had no Brakes –
It was up to the Team and Driver

Gordy said: " just keep talkin' to 'em –
they know how to do this better than you"

That they did and we made many trips to the barn.

What hay we couldn't move,
we stacked in the field
like Pale Green Gum Drops

June 14, 1973

Dear Dad, Marci, Lee and everyone,

It is evening and a long hard work day is past. I spent most of the day in the kitchen cooking food and organizing all the utensils etc. You might find it interesting- for 4 days now it has been in the 100°, the highest 103° Wow I have never lived in such heat ~
3 or 4 trips to the stream to cool off. We are gauging our time and work so that much garden work is done early in the morn and later in the even – the cool parts of the day, even though much work gets done in the middle. How is the weather there? We are in the middle of haying now. Gordy has taught us how to cut and rake with the mules, and shock and stack it. Very hard but rewarding.

There is a doe and fawn living nearby. I saw them early in the morning yesterday- the fawn tottering along and giving suck to the mother
– very far out. Each day is more beautiful, uncovering many levels of life.

The wiki- up becomes more and more comfortable~
I layed down hay and blankets and feel like a bird in a nest. I haven building and ploughing, haying and singing a lot.

Saturday night some of us went to Creston for a community sing. Banjos fiddles country music.
 Lee ~ you would have really loved it. I thought of you.

They really enjoyed our songs so we are invited back next month. Wonderful people- mostly older and very warm and friendly. There are some more young people like us moving in all around and we are all excited at the idea of a big community of farms and people doing the same thing.

Chocolate our cow is getting very pregnant as I'm sure you are Marci (no comparison though – you don't have horns!) 5 more hens are setting so we'll have more chicks.

Getting weary and time for slumber- we cut hay in the morning- a Big Hard Job.

Please write me more letters, I would really like to know how you All are and what you are doing.

I love you all
and sending some surplus heat (in trade for a fan or air conditioning-
one that runs by water we don't have electricity!)

Love,
John

THE CRESTON COMMUNITY SING

...can't remember how exactly we were invited to
this Monthly Event
It was held in the Community Center,
in the town of Creston,
on the Route 5 of Wirt County
about 20 miles to the northwest from The Farm
Friday Nights
and soon became The Centerpiece for our Days
What Songs to Sing, What Clean Clothes to wear,
what Food to bring, what Songs to Sing
Bath night became Thursday night

Rehearsals in the Big Room in the Big House
at Night and on Rainy Days.
What Songs to sing – What Tunes to play
Of course, there was the "Almost Heaven" song,
and my Traditionals,
Eloise was good with the Gospel and Fiddle tunes,
Josh and Tom with the Woody Guthries,
Gerry with the Dylan
We could Always finish with "Will the Circle Be.."

In the beginning, we had no idea what to expect,
Not a Clue and I admit I was pretty nervous.
Well, we caused quite the Stir
when the bunch of us came the door.

Up on Stage, The local talent was shining.
Women Vocal Trios, a girl with an Autoharp.
A young boy with a guitar as big as him
and a voice even bigger.

Then we played our bunch of Tunes and Songs:
"Almost Heaven" first / "Will the Circle" last
I love how the Magic of Music works

Our Big Surprise was when
a Quartet got up to play.
Pure Backwoods Bluegrass
Absolutely blew my socks off.
I was aware of Bluegrass thanks to Earl Scruggs
and the Hee Haw T.V. Show
But THIS!

4 totally un-asuming guys each one a
Master at the instrument
There was the 6' 5" 5- string Banjo player "Rimer"
The Mandolin player Dennis
was still in High School
- his speed and precision numbed me
Tom the Singer/Guitar player who later would
teach me a bunch of songs he sang
Ralph the Bass player smoked cigars.

I really loved the "After the Set" rendezvous
out back of the hall where cigarettes were smoked,
the whisky bottle was passed around
and the music soared

It's When and Where we were Really Welcomed
into the West Virginia Community

Over the following years...
we would perform as the:
"Armadillo Family Band and Theatre Company"

playing Libraries, Benefits and Gatherings in and
around Calhoun County

...and wouldn't miss the Monthly Creston Sing.

June 22, 1973

Dear Marci, Lee and everyone,
        I just received a letter from
Dad and his exclamation of new
"Territory" and a reminder that I forgot to
remind myself to remember to let you
know I received the books in wonderful
shape and to send my "Thank You's" (which
is a common Johnny Lyons error) But.
Nonetheless, I send you my "thank you's"
now.
I have completed Walden- which I
devoured in two rainy days between
building a table for the kitchen. It was
wonderful. I read passages every now and
then from the Bible~ altho at times I've
tried many times to read it as a novel~ it
becomes too heavy so I suffice to casual
reading.
Thank you very much – I think of you
often and wonder how your "belly" is
doing~ I've heard it (the baby) referred to
as an inner tube. How's your inner tube?
HA
        Things on the farm are busy- hay (the
first cutting) is in...garden is growing very
well and we all are healthy and tan faced.
I believe I've never been as brown as I am
right now.

It is nite-time in the woods now
        Fire-flies are incredible and
everywhere.
The Whipoorwill sings all night. I will send
some more poetry along when I finish
editing and smoothing rough edges.
        I have written a lot, but I am still on
the first page and stages.
        Keep a smile in Scottsville for me.
                I love you all,
                        Farmer John

 p.s. A barn swallow family in our barn
                had four babies the other day
        they are very cute
                        see you end of July
                some plans have changed

when I know more I will relate.

June 25, 1973

Dear Dad, Marci, Lee....? , and everyone

In the last letter I said I would be coming in July but now the plans have been reversed and back to the original or a little later. I got the invitation to sing on Long Island Aug. 5 then I will visit with Karen & Mike in CT. for a couple of days, then a friend in Woodstock. So, around Aug. 15th or so I should be at your door. But try not to make too definite a plan if you are at all OK with that?

We are invited to sing at Creston next weekend- we'll be in the papers and all! I'll send you a clipping.

Garden is growing well. We are harvesting lettuce and spinach already.

Keep the letters coming and I will call you when I get to town,
I love you all,

Brother, Son, John

July 25, 1973

Dear Kin.

A wet and restful day at the farm ~ past few days a lot of heavy work got done. Last night about 10 of us went to town to a local beer joint – the bartender really looked surprised and bewildered, but he was very friendly
and we all had a good time
~ seems like everywhere we go people know us- it's nice I guess.
Well, getting ready to travel ~ going to see a lot of things - it's been 5 months here in the valley ~ contact with the outside world will be startling and strange I'm sure but looking forward to it a whole lot. Seeing museums and paintings and places ~ I want to see the mountains and the ocean ~ well it's time for lunch.
I'll be sending postcards along the way, see 'ya in a couple of weeks
Love,
Johnny

Pilgrimaages

This title was influenced by Geoffrey Chaucer's
Canterbury Tales – The General Prologue

"Than longen folk to go on pilgrimages,
And palmers for seken straunge strondes,
To ferne halwes, couthe in sondry londes;
And specially, from every shires ende
of Engelond, to Caunterbury they wende...

It was at the End of July 1973, I ventured out
(after 5 months on the farm in Rowles Run)
to have some Adventures, see a bit of the World
and spend time with Dad and the family.
Along the way, Visit Camden NJ
and Whitman's House,
College friends had invited me to come to their
wedding in Long Island and sing some songs.
Visit My oldest sister Karen, husband Mike and
their daughter Tracey who were living in
Bridgeport Ct.,
before heading to Dad's house near Rochester.
The Plan was to Hitch-hike most of the way. I
studied the maps nightly and came up with:

The Route:

Leave from Parkersburg W. Va. on highway 119
and head East for Washington D.C.
Visit The National Gallery
and an exhibit of Flemish painter Vermeer
From D.C. - travel up North to
Camden, New Jersey and visit Mickle Street.
Walt Whitman's House - National Monument
(I had a friend and old college neighbor
who lived in Camden)

From there, More Up North to N.Y.C
– Long Island - the Wedding
Over to Huntington, Long Island to visit
Whitman's Birthplace,
Up to Port Jefferson to hop
the Ferry over to Bridgeport Ct.
The Final leg – Over and Across New York State
to Dad in Rochester

The Sondry Londes

With Bag packed, Guitar Cased, and
"Emergency" Monies tucked away
I hit Highway 119 out of Parkersburg.

The very First ride was in a Van full of Hippies ~
just like me
"Goin' to the Festival?"
"What Festival?"
"The Bluegrass Festival! - Where've ya been?"
I told my story as we rolled down the road.

My Very First Bluegrass Festival &
It Changed My Life.

* Strondes = Foreign Shores; ferne halwes = Distant
Shrines ;
couthe in sondry londes = know in Sundy Lands

Bluegrass and Beyond
Elkins, West Viginia

I was no stranger to Bluegrass,
Thanks all due to the Creston Family Sings.
Rimer – file 5 string banjo player,
Little James – a 15 year old
Phenomenal Mandolin player, and
Thomas – 6 string Guitar player –
they all took me in the fold
and learned me songs...real good!

My eyes and ears were about to be blown open
tho', that weekend.

The   performers I remember:
The Earl Scruggs Revue
featuring his sons Gary and Randy
with the Legendary Vassar Clemens.
I crossed paths with Earl
as we stood in line for a cup of coffee,
bought him a cup and we chatted briefly –
A Soft Spoken Fine Gentleman. Fine
The Music was Finer and Ledgendary.
Doc Watson was there with his son Merle

My new friends from the Van, Told me
about *The New Grass Revival*

How they take Rhythms from Contemporary
music and Blend them into Bluegrass
Reggae – Gospel – Rock & Roll – Bluegrass
and of the Mandolin/ Fiddle player Sam Bush –
champion fiddler at age 12
and because he breaks so many mandolin strings
while playing,
his wife Lynn, sits on stage changing strings and
swapping out instruments
… and how Bill Monroe refuses to share the stage
with them.
Revolutionary Music Live on Stage

(little did I know at the time, but 10 years later,
we would meet up several times in
Santa Fe, Albuquerque and Telluride)

With my Mind Blown, My Heart Full
and Miles yet to go,

One of my "Van" friends knew
someone who was headed right into downtown

Washington D.C.

Magic Happens

Monangahela and Appalachia

The most I recall are the feelings of how
Immensely Beautiful
the Appalachian Mountain Range and the
Monongahela forests are

Monangahela National Forest East to the Appalachian Range*

Names tumble like a Waterfall :
Monangahela
(Native Unami Tribe = Falling Banks)
Sea Run, Appalachian Plateau, Crystilline
Appalachian Range, The Blue Ridge mountains,
Shenandoah River and the Shenandoah Valley and
the Piedmont Plateau

The Great Wagon Road.
Echos of Horse, Oxen and Wagon.
Ghosts of Stonewall Jackson, Jubal Early, Phillip
Sheridan
and the Boys in Grey and the Boys in Blue.
A Distinctive Blue Green Hush among the Peaks
and Valleys.

Shock of Cultures

After 5 Months living surrounded by 300 acres,
15 people, a Cow, 2 Mules, a Draft Mare
a Flock of chickens and a Wild Mallard Duck,

I was Not prepared for the Teeming Metropolis of
Washington D.C.

Highway Traffic, Speed, Congestion, Noise,
Dozens of Directions

and Thousands of Humans,

All at Once.

In December 1873 (after having his Wallet stolen
in Philadelphia) Walt Whitman arrived in
Washington D.C.
This is what he wrote:

*We all know the chorus: Washington, dusty, muddy,
tiresome Washington is the most awful place, political and
other; is the rendezvous of the national universal axe-
grinding, caucusing, and of our never-ending ballot-chosen
shysters, and perennial smouchers, and windy bawlers from
every quarter far and near. We learn, also, that there is no
society, no art, in Washington; nothing of the elaborated*

high-life attractions of the charming capitals (for rich and morbid idlers) over sea. Truly this particular sort of charm is not in full blossom here; N'IMPORTE. *Let those miss it who miss it, (we have a sad set among our rich young men,) and, if they will, go voyage over sea to find it. But there are man's studies, objects here, nevermore exhilarating ones. What themes, what fields this national city affords, this hour, for eyes of live heads, and for souls fit to feed upon them!*

W.W. NYT 1863*

Walt Whiman Archives - https://whitmanarchive.org/

Walt came to care for his Brother George,
wounded in the Battle of Fredricksburg.

He left for Camden 10 Years later.

I only came for a couple of days to Visit the
National Gallery and see Vermeer
and take a look around.

My New Friend dropped me at a
"Hostel" on the North of the City
- "Q" street. , and not too far
from the City Center.
The following morning, I stowed my guitar and
Pack with the Hostel
and just started walking South.

Now "Q" street was not in the "best" part of town I soon realised as I passed several houses with pretty women all Cat- Calling me from the front porches. It took me by surprise and after a moment – just tipped my hat and continued on my way – just a bit flattered. The little money I had was still secure.

I really had no desire to tourist gawk and didn't care much for crowds of people, I figured I'll just take a look around. I wasn't too far down the road when I came to Ford's Theater. I knew my Dad would love some mementos and decided to take the "tour".

I remembered Dad got a Book for Christmas in 1965:

"The Assasination of Abraham Lincoln"

The book fascinated the both of us. The Stories,
The Photographs, The Tragedy haunts me still.

Like everything in D.C. - The Theatre, the
Boarding House across 10th Street,
all seemed so small.

I continued South to the National Gallery to my
date with The Girl with the Pearl Earring

Requited Love

Growing up, I had a very limited exposure to the
"Fine Arts" and wasn't until I met Jude Binder
        an incredible artist in her own right
She was a Prima Ballerina from Austin, Texas and
a dear lover and friend for many years.
She opened the door for me to the wonders of
Vermeer, Degas, Chagall, Monet, Turner and
Pissarro to name a few.
        I carried a PostCard of "The Pearl Earring"
for years.
To sit in it's aura, was tender and moving – I
wanted to somehow crawl into the frame.
        And she was not alone. There were other
paintings as well: "The Little Street", The Music
Lesson and A Lady Writing a Letter.
        …again, everything seemed so small

Annapolis Detour

I really Do Not Remember how it happened but it
probably was the guy who I rode with
from the Festival... but I ended up going with him
to an Open Mike Session in Annapolis.

I had a quick tour of the City and Look at Naval
Academy and the Vice Principle Residence.
It was 1973 – Spiro Agnew was living there.
But not for long- by Years End
he was forced to resign
from Extortion, Bribery and Tax Evasion charges
while Governor of Maryland.
Republican to the Bone

I played and sang, had a Grand Time
in this quite casual bar setting,
was even invited back to play again
and unlike Ol' Spiro – and left town $30 richer
Enough for a Bus Ticket to Camden
- and then some.

After a night on my friends couch, he dropped me
off at the Greyhound Station

Headed North to New Jersey

Travel Note:

It never really occurred to me until I was in the
Middle of Washington D.C.
How Daunting, Dangerous and Difficult it would
be to Hitchhike.
I was just 23,
Fearless and Pretty Naive.
Traveling with a Guitar
gave me a kind of Legitimacy
Still, I needed to Heed the Voices in my Head
and Proceed Accordingly.
...and Greyhound Bus Service was pretty
convenient and affordable

From Washington D.C. to Camden N.J.
Northeast Thru Baltimore
About 150 miles and a 3+ hour trip
1973 Bus Fare = $20.00 or so

Camden, New Jersey

Once I arrived,
I connected with my College Friends
– got a swift tour of the town,
which was really a huge city
that began in Baltimore
(and Didn't Stop until I reached the North Shores
of Long Island).
'Had a Fun New Jersey Bar -B - Que that night,
with Songs and Stories around a campfire.
The Next morning, now 4 of us, in a little blue car
were off to The Whitman house.

326 Mickle Street

"Walt Whiman Archives - https://whitmanarchive.org/ "

We weren't aware Mickle St. had been re- named
to Martin Luther King Blvd., so it took us awhile
to   find it and giving me a chance to see
the territory, which was a prime example of Urban
Plight and quite run down. My friends were
more concerned than I was, and not really keen on
taking "the tour", so they dropped me off with the
plan to pick me up an hour later.

The Pope of Mickle Street

Walt bought the house in 1884 for $1,750 and a
year later was living with Mary Oakes Davis as his
house keeper, alone with her spotted Dog
"Watch":

"He is the nastiest, noisiest, silliest, stupidest,
horriblest dog that was ever born
a pest, a continual sore in my side! He howls a
hundred times a day, at all hours .
In the night, too, generally about one o'clock when
the rest of the world wants to keep quiet"

There was a Methodist Church Nearby
and it's Bell and a choir
with an "unsettling band of singers"
which didn't seem to improve
despite the constant practice.

There were the Marching Bands in warm weather:
"Oh! The Bands out in the street- the drum and
fife corps that rattling and banging past:
        they beat my miserable head like hammers."
And then in 1888, a pianist took up daily practice
sessions nearby.
He called his house "The Shanty"

Present Day 1973, the house (like everything)
seemed so small.

Musty and Dark, I was greeted by Mary Oakes
Davis herself – or so I thought.
No warm welcome here, the lady I met must've
been in her 80's, and a manner to boot.
She curtly gave me the "Guided Tour" -
1st Floor Parlor and the Backrooms.
Up the narrow stairway to the 2nd Floor
The Front Rooms were Walt's, with his Large
Rocking Chair, a Table, Chairs
and the Corded off Bedstead where he made his
'Transition".

I had never been in such a "Powerful Space" in my
days.

I was not allowed to touch anything.
Though I DID manage to rest my hand on his rocker.

"Walt Whiman Archives - https://whitmanarchive.org/"

The "tour" lasted but a half-hour, I hungout across the street and wrote this:

Outside of Mickle Street

What was it you whispered me, on the front steps?
In front, the Sycamore full grown,
Cobblestone street tarred over
The once travelled over cobblestone street
Hoofprints and carriage whips
Sound of iron wheelrims on cobblestone
Sycamore autumn'd leaves and wind
Hands in coat pockets, wide lapelled and the tanned
Hat notched north
"Expecting rain today..."
was all I caught with my ears
the rest,
dropped on the walk
Or was carried to the river where
you frequented.

(Words written by Johnny Lyons outside Walt Whitman's house
— Mickle Street, Camden, NJ 1973)

Paumanauk
(Native American name for Long Island)

Isle of sweet brooks of drinking-water—healthy air and soil!
Isle of the salty shore and breeze and brine! - W.W. 1880

Bidding my Camden friends a *Fare – thee – Well,*
I boarded another Greyhound Bus headed North
for New York City and a Connection to
the Long Island Railroad.
The further North I went the Greater the Tangle
of Highways, By-ways,
Railroads, Asphalt and Pavements, Bridges and
Underpasses
I am amazed how I navigated such
through it all...at all.
I had to figure out the Long Island Rail System to
get me to the Wedding in Hempstead first:
The Rest will follow.
It was My friend Beth's Wedding and was
Celebrated at her house.
My very First Wedding Gig - it was lovely in the
Suburban Hempstead Backyard
Tiki Torches were ablaze in the evening and Songs
aplenty drifted through the neighborhood.

The West Hills

By the next morning, I was on the rails again
headed Northeast
for the West Hills of Huntington, and the
Whitman Homestead.

It took a Huge amount of Imagining, to envision
what it looked like in the 1820's
when all around me were Highways, Buildings,
Neighborhoods and:

I had been warned, But Still.

Threading my way Over Asphalt and Under
Overpasses, I found
the Old Whitman Homestead,
Quiet and Serene amongst it all,
nestled on a small hill.
I had arrived early and had to wait for the caretaker
to arrive, I found a shade to rest and wait
All the while, feeling like I've been un-ravelling
time and wrote this :

West Hills, Huntington

"Walt Whiman Archives - https://whitmanarchive.org/ "

I sit on the curb'd front of the house
you were born in, my brother
touching the green grass and white clover
and close trimmed timothy,
where your spirit breathes.

Days ago I stood by the window where
you sat idly by,
rested my eyes on the bed where you were
born-again. I feel you in these places.
Oh but much more so along the banks
and runs- underneath the Cedar boughs
and freshly fruited persimmon.

Taking backward and sideward glances,
curious as to what might come next.
I wait for the woman who tends
your birthhome.
Much is changed now as you well know.

After a tour of the house (which was a quaint old
Farm house) I didn't feel any sparks and I needed
to backtrack some, catch the Train to Port
Jefferson, then catch the ferry North.
across Long Island Sound to Bridgeport
Connecticut, my sister Karen and her family.

There was a huge tug of war in me because I kinda sorta I Really wanted to go to Montauk Point another 100 miles East – way out on the very Tip of Long Island. The Very Tip!

FROM MONTAUK POINT.

I stand as on some mighty eagle's beak,
Eastward the sea absorbing, viewing,
(nothing but sea and sky,)
The tossing waves, the foam, the ships in the distance
The wild unrest, the snowy, curling caps- that inbound
urge and urge of waves,
seeking the shores forever,
W.W Sands at Seventy

if you go Directly East- 3,374 Miles – you can have dinner in Lisbon, Portugal

but not as a good as my sisters home cookin' and I
was pretty weary at this point,
having been on the road for over a week

A Ride on a Ferry looked pretty good to me

The Ferry lay waiting for me at the port

I had never been on a Ferry before, let alone across
a large body of water.

The largest I ever knew was Lake Ontario
where I went swimming as a kid at a relatives
cottage in the summer,
and drinking beer on the shore after Senior Prom.

The Long Island Sound is really a Tidal Estuary
18 Rivers pour into it from Quebec through New
England down to Connecticut

From 65' to 230 feet deep

18 miles across and the Ferry Ride just a bit over
an hour to Bridgeport

Cost = $8

Connecticut

Everywhere I looked, it was quite evident I had
arrived in New England.

The Spaces were so different from Long Island.
The Light Brighter, The Air Cleaner.
The Quaint.

I totally enjoyed my visit with Karen, Mike and
Two Year Old Tracey.
The tale lives on to this day that
I ate more Meat than the Law allowed,
especially since I had Declared
over a year ago I was Vegetarian

Here is the One poem that survived:

A Song Written on a High Wall Overlooking ConnecticutLand

I stand above you Connecticut
Overlooking your Blueish hills
Rolling and Stretching to the sea.
I crossed over your knee-high stone fences
- some hundreds of years old toppledover and new vines
cement them
where they have fallen.

I sit in the ashes of a burnt down house
charcoal black and gray.
I see your pines that stand aloft
the Oak and Bitch and Maple
one the hillside facing the hillside where I sit.
I see the nests of the many birds,
hear the cry of the Crow and chirp of Sparrow
a Cardinal's teeet
chuckle of squirrel — a nest high in the Birch
I watch for movement , more than the wind
I watch a Dazzling sun fall behind your hills,
to throw colors western up into sky.

All too soon, I was aboard a Greyhound Bus
headed West to Rochester, Scottsville and Dad
350 miles West   5+ hours
New York State Thruway 90
The last time I rode the Thruway was in 1969
headed to Woodstock
The Thruway has a special place in my heart — as it
parallels the Erie Canal
and travels all the way to Buffalo.

Years later it would inspire me to write one of my
favorite songs:

Fine Times Carve Fine Lines
1975

Will you hold me
Won't you stone me
Will you stay with me tonight
I'll hold you
and I'll stone you
and press you to my side

ch: The rivers
Thru the valleys
Rollin' just as slow
Erie Canal
Schenectady
I'm packed up for Buffalo

There's a Train runnin' down the track
She's a Beamin' throught the rain
'Feel that She's a- carrying that
Ol' Hobo round again

chorus

I've been riding down the highway
Findin's songs in Every Place
and Fine Times Carve Fine Lines
On my Hands and On My Face

chorus

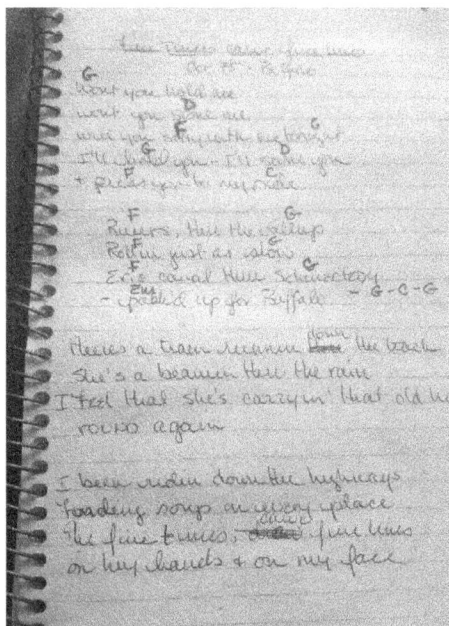

Scottsville

1973 – Population 1,801
Photo credit: https://www.scottsvilleny.org

About 15 miles South from Brighton, New York –
where we lived in the '60's.
It was Way out in country to my young eyes. We
all would visit Dad's youngest sister Janet,
her husband "Uncle Bub" and his son Kirk -3
years younger than me.
Uncle Bub designed and built his house on a
prominent corner on the edge of town.
My sister Marci, husband Lee and months old
daughter, Sarah had been living here for
several years and – settled Dad
in the town, to be closer to them.

32 Rochester Street

Photo credit: https://www.scottsvilleny.org

To this day, I remain confused
There's: The Village of Scottsville, which is in the
Town of Wheatland which is in Monroe County
and they call the school district
"Wheatland - Chili"
and you have to travel thru Henrietta to get
there....

Scottsville's Main Drag

Surrounded by Sweet Corn Fields, Dairy Farms,
Wheat Fields, Horse Farms,
Gardens in every yard and Streets
lined with Century Old Trees.
All watered by the Mighty Genessee River and the
Gentle Oatka Creek.
A Lovely Town

Dad rented a Small, One Bedroom Attached
Apartment on the Main Drag - Rochester Street
The bedroom was Up- stairs with the Living room,
Dining/ Common Room
and tiny Kitchen downstairs. It was smaller than a
Galley on a Tugboat.
I think the only time the two of us danced,
was in that room.
He had a wee cot set up in the "Common" room
for me to sleep, and set my pack and Guitar.
Cozy, Close   just like the two of us.

I took no notes, did not journal during my stay, but
I do remember walking into town
to do the shops with him pulling a little wire basket
on wheels for the packages
and introducing me to EVERYONE in the Town.
From Shorty at the Market, to Beanie at the Fire
House. to Boomer at the Post Office
to the Library to the Bowling Alley and

The Greeks Lounge, The Corner Diner
And the word spread - "There's a Bearded Long
Haired Hippie in Town"

Between our dancing in the kitchen, and soirees to
town, we spent time with Marci, Lee and Sarah
There was Monty Python on PBS Sunday Nights,
singing him the New songs I wrote, telling him the
tales I'm telling you and simply being together.
Sometimes I'd wander downtown with my guitar
looking for a spot to park and play.
I soon found out,
the bench outside the library was not cool.
I think folks were afraid of me?
What I represented?

After few weeks, it was time
to head back to the farm.
It was Harvest Season now,
All hands on Deck

I boarded a Greyhound Once More

This time Southbound via Buffalo and back to
"West By God" Virginia
8 hours   420 Miles   To Go

Piecing together All the miles Traveled on this 6 week Pilgrimages?

1,350 mi

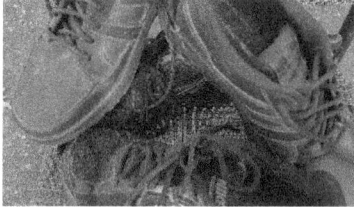

.......a photo of those shoes

October 5 1973

Dear Dad, Marci, Lee and darlin'
Sarah,

Hello hello from down here in West
Virginia. Every mountain now has colours
galore and new colors every morning. This
morning I went groundhog hunting with
no luck at all. Sometime I know I'll see the
one who has been eating our cantaloupes
and watermelons. It has been raining for
two days- the West Virginia monsoons
have begun. Today has been windy and
blue skies – a very lovely Autumn day.
I have been reading a lot of different
books recently. A book about the Shakers
who were a religious communal group in
Early America Here's a beautiful passage:

"We believed we were debtors to God
in relation to each other, and all men, to
improve our time and talents in this life, in
that manner in which we might be most
useful."   Shaker Covenant, 1795

Also I have been reading a history of
West Virginia and a long narrative poem
"Western Star" - Stephan Vincent Benet.
Just to break up my time I read from a

Buddhist Treatise - The Diamond Sutra and The Sutra of Hui Neng. It has some enlightening thoughts on God and The Universe which are good to think about when I work.

I've been working on the Root Cellar mostly building shelves and bins to store food. After I finish that I'll be putting a roof on another root cellar by the little house and shelving that also.
Our carrots didn't do so well this year but we have a lot of Beets and Rutabagas. Which will make up for them. I've started to collect apple seeds to germinate this winter so we can begin an orchard- it takes 3 years to grow before it produces fruit- so it's a long term project.

~ have had some interesting visitors -

- Bobby's parents from N.Y.C. To stay for a few days- they are your age and very wonderful people.

- A lady came from the Parkersburg paper to write an article about us. There were conflicting feelings about it though. Some feel, like I do that some people who read the story will be hostile to people like us-

"Communal Hippies" is a term or category they put us in. Some people are just plain curious. So for our notoriety, we are expecting "tourists", No address was given, but if people want to find us, they can. I'm not too worried , but cautious and careful none-the-less. When we get the paper -I will send.

— There are two beautiful ladies here from a commune in Tick Creek Tennessee. They are real nice and very well read in Astrology. They run around asking people when they were born- then OOO and AHH. They made my astrological chart but I don't know what it means from a Groundhog Hole in the ground.

— Gordy is out of the hospital and staying with his daughter in Creston. It seems most of the people in this area are very heavy into alcohol. It felt real good to help Gordy get well.

You were asking when I'll be home for X-mas?

We are having a Wedding on Winter Solstice (Dec.23). So I'll be leaving here on the 23rd and be home Christmas Eve. I'd like to take the Bus providing I earn the money before then. It will be much easier taking the Bus in the winter than hitch-hiking.

We have already begun Wood Runs for winter- Ugh!
How is Sarah Catherine- I think of her very often – she must be Beautiful! (A touch of Irish eh?)
Dad – I hope you are feeling better and taking good care of yourself. I take you into my heart every morning and pray that you stay well.
Give my regards to the neighbors and friends in Scottsville- Aunt Jan – Uncle Bub, Kirk and the Loomis Folks too. Enjoy the Autumn and her colours.
There will be a package coming soon.
I love you all muchly,
Son and Brother Johnny

please send me Grammies address- I going to give her some pictures

October 20 1973

Dear Dad and Folks,
 *Hope Marci got her package from me –
let me know if she hasn't. Everything is
fine and wet here. Straight Cold Rain and
wet here for 2 straight days and probably
tomorrow too – Ugh_ it really slows down
the work schedule. Haven't gotten it
together to find out the costs and times of
the Bus lignes to up there but will soon and
let you know.*
 *I lost Grammies address AGAIN- oh
my, the last time I saw it was in my back
pocket! Oh My, how's the weather up
north? - Any snow?*
 *I love you all and our cow gives 5
gallons -a -day!!!*
 Stay warm and dry for me,
  Love Johnny Lion
(that's what all the little kids here call me!)

November 7 1973

Hello Hello to All,

It's been so very busy here getting ready for the Onslaught of Winter Cold Weather. If y'all think about it ~ it's a whole lot different when cold weather means a tight leak proof house and plenty of cut hard – dry wood.... Wood runs every day – into the woods with the mules and hauling logs down off the ridges. Plenty of chopping! It snowed Saturday a little – so very beautiful. I thought of New York State.

This weekend we sang and played at 2 different places – a Benefit for the Creston Community Building - playing with the local Bluegrass Band- they like me to sit in with them. All of them are in their 40's and such good musicians – they have taught me a lot. More and More people from the area want us to come and sing at their places for benefits etc. The "Farm" is getting well known and accepted as part of the community – even the Dentist comes!

Here is the article about us. One thing I ask is for 2 dozen copies for everybody's folks and Grandparents etc.. This is the Only Copy we have.

Thinking of Thanksgiving...what's everyone doing up there? Lots of friends are coming here to visit- and we'll be having feasts (hopefully some Wild Grouse or Pheasant – if the woods are kind)

It's 9 pm and an early day tomorrow – rebuild the kitchen.

Hope everybody's fine and warm
Johnny

Note – No copies of the newspaper article mentioned were found on the World Wide Web.

November ? 1973

Hello Again to One and All,
        Very tired tonight. I have been on
"House" today ....cooking and cleaning.
Made rice- cream cereal with milk for
breakfast, last night's leftover rice casserole
for lunch. Dinner, I made baked potatoes,
lentil soup, tomato casserole and
sauerkraut. Alot of dishes to wash
afterwards... for 15 people. Can you
imagine? Here is a newspaper
article...hope you enjoy and please make
copies to send down. I had another idea for
Xmas . A copy of the

        I-CHING
            or
        Book of Changes

Clear warm
weather here
have you heard
  about the comet?
 Or have you seen it yet?
        Write some letters -
        Love,
                    Johnny

Hello again to one and all.
Very tired tonight. I have been at house today... cooking and cleaning,
made nice cream cereal for breakfast with milk, last nights left?
over nice casserole for lunch. Dinner, I made bake potatoes,
lentil soup, tomato casserole and sauerkraut, a lot of dishes
to wash after meals... for 15 people can you imagine? Here is
the newspaper article... I hope you enjoy & please make copies to
send down. I had another idea for X mas. a copy of the
        I CHING
             or
        Book of Changes
the Richard Wilhelm Translation
rendered into English by Cary F. Baynes
        foreword by C. G. Jung
    Bollingen Series XIX   Princeton University Press 1950
                                    (7.50)
Clear summer
weather here
have you heard
    about the comet?
or have you seen it yet?
                Write me some Jetty -
            Love Johnny

November 29 1973

Hello Hello to All,

It's been so very busy here getting ready for the Onslaught of Winter Cold Weather. If y'all think about it ~ it's a whole lot different different when cold weather means a tight leak proof house and plenty of cut hard - dry wood....Wood runs every day - into the woods with the mules and hauling logs down off the ridges. Plenty of chopping! It snowed Saturday a little - so very beautiful. I thought of New York State.

This weekend we sang and played at 2 different places - a Benefit for the Creston Community Building - playing with the local Bluegrass Band- they like me to sit in with them. All of them are in their 40's and such good musicians - they have taught me a lot. More and More people from the area want us to come and sing at their places for benefits etc. The "Farm" is getting well known and accepted as part of the community - even the Dentist comes!

Here is the article about us. One thing I ask is for 2 dozen copies for everybody's folks and Grandparents etc.. This is the Only Copy we have.

Thinking of Thanksgiving...what's everyone doing up there? Lots of friends are coming here to visit- and we'll be having feasts (hopefully some Wild Grouse or Pheasant - if the woods are kind)

It's 9 pm and an early day tomorrow - rebuild the kitchen.

Hope everybody's fine and warm

Johnny

December 15, 1973

Dear Dad and Kin.

    Big Howdy hello from down here.
Winterizing is coming long after a Festive
Thanksgiving.
I have the information as to the Buses
    It costs $ 28.63 from Spenser W. Va to
There
    Arrival time 3:30 in Rochester on
Christmas Eve (subject to change)
  I will call you along the way to let you
know when exactly on the hour
... sure am happy to know I'll be with you
all ~really looking forward to it
Hope all is well and drop a line when you
can
        `that's about all,
          muchly,
            Son John

I made it back up to Dad, Family and the Scottsville
Christmas Eve with plenty of celebrations
                    ... didn't get back down to the the farm until
mid January.
            From this perspective, Forty Years Later
        looking back from April to December – 9 Months
                    What an Incredible Journey
                        and there's MORE!

1974 and More Adventures Await Around the Corner

Enjoy a Musical Playlist
"Rowell's Run"
Songs we Sang And Loved
On SPOTIFY

Go Raibth Maith Agat to:

Orris the Mailman of Star Route
To Marci & Lee for Being There and Helping to Save The
Folder of Letters
The Amazing Cast of "Pilgrimaages"
The Walt Whitman Archives for the Photos and Quotes
– it's an amazing treasure
David S. Reynolds - "Walt Whitman's America"
The Miscellaneous Photo's I have sprinkled about and
around are from:
"The Worldwide Information Super Highway"
I did look for names, and found none,
so if there's a photo of yours- Thanks!
And of course, So Many Thank You's
to Karla Meyer of "2 Pups"
for making the Journey possible!

The Story on the Cover

In one of the letters was a wee bundle of my hair from a
trim I had.
Dad was not fond of my locks flowing down my back.
I knew this would make him happy...

Love Breeds Forbearance surely
- jwl

www.ingramcontent.com/pod-product-compliance
Lightning Source LLC
Chambersburg PA
CBHW031602040426
42452CB00006B/383